Rediscovering Our Future
The Modern Liberal Arts Education Manifesto
2015, First Edition

Chris Draper, Ph.D., P.E.

PRESS

Copyright © 2015 by EmergeHUB Company

All rights reserved. This book or any portion thereof may not be reproduced or used in any manner whatsoever without the express written permission of the publisher except for the use of brief quotations in a book review.

First Edition, 2015

ISBN-13: 978-0692542408 (The Press)

ISBN-10: 069254240X

Published in the United States by:

4225 Fleur Drive #132 | Des Moines, Iowa 50321

No one notices a two-degree shift. And it only takes ninety of them to turn the boat around.

Forward

> "Liberal Education is an approach to learning that empowers individuals and prepares them to deal with complexity, diversity, and change. It provides students with broad knowledge of the wider world (e.g., science, culture, and society) as well as in-depth study in a specific area of interest. A liberal education helps students develop a sense of social responsibility, as well as strong and transferable intellectual and practical skills such as communication, analytical and problem-solving skills, and a demonstrated ability to apply knowledge and skills in real-world settings."
>
> –Association of American Colleges and Universities, 2015

Attacks have been levied against liberal arts education for centuries. Attacks are often *industrial*, claiming a liberal arts education does not prepare its graduates for the workplace; *purist*, claiming the study of anything directly relevant to job training is antithetical to liberal education; or *populist*, claiming that a liberal arts education should be accessible to anyone. None of these attacks are baseless, yet all demonstrate a blatant misunderstanding of the unique value of a liberal arts education.

The intensity of these attacks increases during seasons when economic prosperity affords access to political populism. The battle between intellectual purity and industrial practicality presented in the Yale Report of

1828, which is often interpreted as a defense of the wider American liberal arts education at a time when both our economic power and Jacksonian democracy were on the rise, seems eerily familiar to the current battle. In the face of significant curricular expansions, the authors express surprise in the public opinion that liberal arts institutions, which are "immovably moored to the same station...serve only to measure the rapid current of improvement which is passing by them." The authors do not, however, conclude that such a curricular expansion may instead be a reactionary symptom of underlying core challenges — core challenges that remain today.

Few of the core challenges to liberal arts education have changed in the 187 years since the publication of the Yale Report of 1828. As liberal arts supporters, we still argue that our liberal arts institutions are too undercapitalized to reform: "All the means which are now applied to the proper collegiate department, are barely sufficient, or rather are insufficient, for the object in view."[1] We still argue that students and parents do not appreciate the value a liberal arts education provides: "We are concerned to find, that not only students, but their parents also, seem frequently more solicitous for the name of an education, than the substance."[2] We still argue that our students are underprepared: "One of the principal of these, is the call which is so frequently made upon us, to admit students into the college with defective preparation."[3] And we

---

[1] The Yale Report of 1828, Page 25
[2] The Yale Report of 1828, Page 27
[3] The Yale Report of 1828, Page 26

continue to struggle for balance in accepting a profitable number of students while adhering to our higher standards:

> "But might we not, by making the college more accessible to different descriptions of persons, enlarge our numbers, and in that way, increase our income? This might be the operation of the measure, for a very short time, while a degree from the college should retain its present value in public estimation; a value depending entirely upon the character of the education which we give...When the college has lost its hold on the public confidence, by depressing its standard of merit, by substituting a partial, for a thorough education, we may expect that it will be deserted by that class of persons who have hitherto been drawn here by high expectations and purposes."[4]

In 1828, a perceived competition with the "many academies in the country, whose scheme of studies, at least upon paper, is more various than that of the colleges"[5] caused this arrival at the false option of depressing standards. Today, while liberal arts institutions often believe they are competing with everything from community colleges to Massive Open Online Courses (MOOCs), business analysts like Moody again cause liberal arts institutions to question their principles:

---

[4] The Yale Report of 1828, Page 25
[5] The Yale Report of 1828, Page 24

"Small private colleges that don't offer what today's students want...are facing potentially devastating financial pressures that can lead to a "death spiral" of declining admissions, tuition revenues, and contributions...Schools that...don't have a "demonstrated return on investment...will face increased competition from cheaper public higher education as well as distance learning options."[6]

Education is commoditized now more than ever. Search engines in a sharing economy have made monopolization of data nearly untenable. This technological commoditization of education positions every human a few clicks away from our world's thought leaders. Any individual can be exposed to any theory at nearly no cost. Most notably, technology is forcing liberal arts institutions to grapple with a world that has commoditized its most recognizable asset: lectures.

Lectures became the cornerstone of a liberal arts education around the year 1050 AD. Nearly 800 years later, the Yale Report of 1828 describes the benefit of a good lecture as having the ability to "give that light and spirit to the subject, which awaken the interest and ardor of the student...[lectures] may place before him the principles of science, in the attractive dress of living eloquence."[7] Students attended great colleges that are

---

[6] Clark, K., Some Small Private Colleges Are Facing a "Death Spiral", *Time Magazine* (online), March 4, 2015, retrieved March 15, 2015: http://time.com/money/3731250/sweet-briar-private-college-death-spiral/
[7] The Yale Report of 1828, Page 10

built upon great lecturers. In institutions where the learning is of greater importance than research and entertainment is the primary means of facilitating learning, the lecture became the institution's primary currency.

Now that lectures are freely traded on the internet through MOOCs and online courses, any student in any college can find and listen to any of the best entertainer-lecturers from anywhere in the world. Despite the fact that new research concludes students in lecture-based courses are 1.5 times more likely to fail than students in courses that are using active learning techniques,[8] it is difficult to imaging a liberal arts institution that does not revolve around lectures. It is probably harder still to remember that liberal education existed for over 1,000 years on tutorial-based methods before the lecture was widely adopted.

There are countless articles and opinion pieces on how to save liberal arts education. These range from calls for "large-scale reform...of general education courses and distribution requirements; the relationship between cultural literacy and learning how to learn; and the degree to which liberal learning really does produce critical thinking," to "studying the great books of world civilization...[for] learning how to live," and "integrating

---

[8] Scott Freemana, Sarah L. Eddy, Miles McDonough, Michelle K. Smith, Nnadozie Okoroafor, Hannah Jordt, and Mary Pat Wenderoth, Active learning increases student performance in science, engineering, and mathematics, *Proceedings of the National Academy of Sciences of the United States of America*, vol. 111 no. 23, 8410–8415

job skills into academic itineraries."[9] Most of these proposals are derivative concepts based on what we know to be a liberal arts education. They are based on institutions that house lectures. They are based on lectures on a particular subject matter. They are based on a concept that students pay for the delivery of data. In contrast, this manifesto takes a first principles approach to exploring the modern liberal arts education.

At its core, a liberal arts education cultivates free human beings.

This manifesto seeks to define what that means in our modern society.

---

[9] Glenn Altschuler, W(h)ither the Liberal Arts?, *The Conversation* (online), April 8, 2015, retrieved on May 15, 2015: http://theconversation.com/w-h-ither-the-liberal-arts-39768

Part I: Focus

Simple problems can have thousands of solutions. Success requires focusing on the reasoning that drives a particular solution. This section will focus on the underlying assumptions we must be willing to call into question.

See the world as it is today.

We live in a post-corporate world, one in which more people are responsible for controlling their own destiny than at any other time since the industrial revolution. Companies are routinely turning employees into independent contractors. Those who stay in the company structure are seeing training budgets slashed and benefits evaporating. "Long term" is quickly turning into eighteen months rather than thirty years. Planning is moving from five year visions to quarterly reports. Rare is the path within one company from the cubicle farm to the corner office. Workers succeed by blazing their own trails through a series of lateral moves, external jumps, and leaps of faith.

At the same time, technology has made data acquisition nearly instantaneous. Millennials are not uniquely technology savvy. Millennials are extraordinarily ignorant of technology. Their use of technology looks like a car mechanic who knows little more than what the diagnostic computer spits out. Both are adept at acquiring a level of data that was unimaginable to generations before. Neither has to wonder about a fact. Neither debates root cause, an exercise that would make their powers of reasoning stronger, when Google or YouTube can provide the answer in nanoseconds. No son or daughter, student, or employee must go to their superior to learn a fact. When a basic fact cannot be found in the Google age, it says more about the researcher's laziness than the amount of available information. And as parents, professors, and employers marvel at their rate of data acquisition, we allow intergenerational tension to grow when we fail to acknowledge the reality that data is not applicable until it is synthesized. Confusing the fundamental differences between data and information obscures the value of a liberal arts education.

Traditional corporate roles are vanishing. The informational barriers, which made traditional libraries, educational institutions, and the majority of corporate research and development divisions necessary, evaporated years ago. The world is a fluid environment of continually evolving alliances. What was once considered traditional business is now front and center in our own lives. Every one of us is the CEO of a "me corporation." We all must learn how to operate in a world where invoicing and billing is the modern equivalent of subsistence farming. We must personally invest our retirement savings, personally manage our health care options, and personally mitigate risk through our insurance choices. Our lives have become our business, and like any business, we must attain a level of knowledge about a broad range of topics so that we understand when and where we need an expert practitioner to take over.

Into the unknown

Our world has always been changing. Look at the big picture: The emergence of switchboard operators was as predictable as their eventual obsolescence. Technological breakthroughs between 1876 through the 1960s took us from creation of the telephone to elimination of the switchboard operator. In that time, generations of workers applied for, held, and retired from that job. From switchboard operators to ice cutters, lamp lighters to log drivers, technology has both continually eliminated and created jobs. Today, the difference is in the pace of this upheaval.

Computer languages live for only a matter of years. Rapid manufacturing shortens procurement lead times from years to minutes. Factories routinely increase production while reducing staff. Technology is creating positions that occupied little more than dreams fewer than 20 years ago. Who would have imagined the existence of a cloud services specialist, a drone pilot, or an Android developer in the 1990s? Where our parents held only a handful of jobs in their lifetimes, we see the entire rise and fall of entire industries during the course of a single career.

Beyond the pace at which the world is changing, our socioeconomic security is not solely attributable to our business relationships. While there was significant corporate upheaval in the 1960s, individuals were largely moved from one professional alliance to another while their professional role and socioeconomic standing remained reasonably consistent. That is no longer the case. Employers are largely helpless to control or even smooth the rate of change. And these changes, more importantly, have the ability to affect every aspect of our lives arbitrarily. From refocusing our efforts to redefining our professional value, these changes are immediate and fundamental.

Adapt or die
Humans have had to "adapt or die" since long before Billy Beane reportedly uttered these words to his scouts. The adaptations may have been smaller, the events may have been better telegraphed, and the lead time may have been longer, but this need has always existed. Now that this need to "adapt or die" is so complete and sudden, we must be cognizant of the fact that successful adaptations require a different kind of preparation. We must remember that there may be no professional crossover or skill transfer. To avoid being physically uprooted, a welder may no longer be able to weld. To avoid being financially uprooted, a middle manager may no longer be able to work as a company man. To avoid being emotionally uprooted, an individual must be able to accept his or her situational impermanence.

It is not the role of the employer to prepare an individual for his or her next step. Some may offer transitional or retraining services, but this is not standard. Our professional benefits no longer linger after our day-to-day relationships are severed. From the moment we separate, we are on our own, and that can be bewildering.

There are plenty of options for gaining specific skills. There are plenty of programs meant to teach professional techniques. There are plenty of options for individuals to become practitioners. But individuals cannot acquire these unless his or her base faculties are suitably honed. These cannot be acquired if the individual is not able to think past that which he or she sees. These cannot be acquired if the individual myopically pursues a limited education in favor of expedience. We will not see, by definition, the next big surprise around the corner, yet we must be ready to tackle it head-on.

The "Left Behind" Generation

The *No Child Left Behind Act* came into effect on January 8, 2002, and the first class of graduates who know no other educational system will soon cross the stage. Designed to create transparent, repeatable accountability, it is often cited as cultivating a culture of teachers who teach to the test. Where scores have improved, others have argued that the standards have been lowered. Regardless of the merits associated with an educational program built around performance on standardized testing, the troubling epicenter of this system is a learned understanding that every question has a correct answer.

We must face this most important reality. It is not that the world is in upheaval. It is not that there is no score at the end of the day. It is not that the world is ambiguous. The most important reality is that we now have an entire generation of emerging adults who believe there is an answer for any and all of it. They think if they wait long enough, someone will tell them which options are right and which are wrong and that if they do nothing, they will not be wrong.

The difficult reality is this: five is rarely less than eight. Both five and eight are objective representations of subjective realities. Humans often use these representations without accounting for their inherent uncertainty because we have trouble accepting the unknown. Yet understanding our context is the key to making meaningful contributions for the betterment of humanity, and a relentless focus on standardized testing throughout the most formative years of our education process, with its dogma of right and wrong, has made appreciating abstractions more difficult. If a student assumes it is suitable to conform to a system of nearly rote learning until he or she has amassed a suitable intellectual base upon which to build true depth into a subject, someone must temper that dependence on artificial datums. Someone must turn this world awash in data into a society driven by information. Someone must explain that the earth is not fixed — that it is continually in motion. Someone must move from an understanding of the idealized world we have constructed for the coming generations to a broadened understanding of the wider world and the universe they are responsible for creating within it.

Our contemporary reality is a world searching for humanity.

Seek the destination.
For more than two millennia, the fundamental purpose of a liberal arts education has remained unchanged: *to enable individuals to take an active role in civic life.* Regardless of form, every technique employed in each

iteration of the liberal arts institution is intended to improve the ability of the institution to facilitate personal discovery. However, in far too many institutions, attempts to "retain its present value in public estimation"[10] have eclipsed the institution's fundamental purpose. In far too many institutions, students are believed to realize value through the degrees bestowed upon them. In far too many institutions, the degree is the destination and the institution is the focus.

There is nothing in the mission of a liberal arts institution that says any degree has any intrinsic value. Mere completion of a mathematics course at a specific college is irrelevant. Value exists only when time at the institution enables the student to become a brilliant mathematician through his or her journey to personal discovery. The collection of majors and minors routinely issued by liberal arts institutions may occupy a handful of lines on a resume, but these lines alone are meaningless without the context of that individual's accomplishments.

Liberal arts institutions routinely boast low faculty to student ratios. These low ratios are ideal for facilitating personal discovery. Within the study of philosophy, having such extraordinary access to professors means each student could have hours of direct, individualized tutorial per standard, forty-hour work week. This access could lead to a highly personalized experience, allowing students to define their own meaning of pursued majors.

---

[10] The Yale Report of 1828, Page 25

Instead, by littering our institutions with more than one major for every five students, we create an environment that rewards the acquisition of institution-specific titles over individualized knowledge.

Fundamentally practical

Purists and reformists have argued for centuries over the appropriate balance between fundamental knowledge and employable skills. The addition of courses focused on professional trades is often seen as counter to the ethos of a liberal arts education. This argument is furthered by the method in which professors teach these professional trades. By competing as miniature universities—arguing that graduates with a particular major can step directly into the advertised profession—liberal arts institutions impair the future earning potential of their graduates. Given the low faculty to student ratio, a liberal arts institution cannot afford to hire experts in the practical application of each professional trade. By underpreparing practitioners, the institution does its graduates a disservice, and by focusing on the preparation of practitioners, it is making a significant strategic error.

Switching focus to the fundamentals that enable an individual to follow nearly any career path is how a liberal arts institution can provide meaningful value. For example, while it is questionable whether the current focus of an undergraduate business degree should fall within the offering of a liberal arts institution, the fundamentals behind a business degree are undoubtedly relevant. Simply put, business is the art of earning enough trust from someone that this someone will give you money. For example, consultants earn trust by assembling a resume that potential customers believe predict the quality of their future work. McDonald's earns trust by making food with such consistency that potential customers know what they will get. Walmart earns trust by optimizing its supply chain to the point that potential customers believe their products will always be cost effective. No matter what specialty is applied to which product, the organization of humans such that they are collectively able to earn the trust of paying customers is the real value, and that value is directly derived from the ability to practically apply the fundamentals of a liberal arts education.

However, as with any human activity, no textbook or software is sufficient for developing a practical grasp of the associated fundamentals. We keep changing as our environment keeps changing. We can read everything that has been written, sit at the feet of experts our whole lives, or watch others work until everything has been done, yet we will not be in any better position to apply this information. The application of these fundamentals is the key to learning. What is truly valuable is experimental safety, which a liberal arts institution provides. The value lies in the ability to be informed by the past while practicing the future. To do this, our liberal arts institutions must focus on the path that enables our discovery, not assume we will have discovered everything by the time we leave. Only by creating a pathway for applying intellectual fundamentals to the practical world will we enable access to the true value of a liberal arts institution.

Obsoletely isolated

These pathways cannot be created if our liberal arts institutions remain ignorant of what is practical. Within academic institutions that see their purpose as preparing individuals for specific roles within a defined workforce, the employers provide specific, integrated guidance and direction. For example, many community colleges operate manufacturing programs using equipment that is provided by and identical to that which is used by the largest local employers. These community colleges are effectively delivering practical skills training that is based on essentially unidirectional communication. But with every economic downturn, or in communities where a particular labor need is already met, the students who thrive in these environments have to go back to the community college. They have to learn everything over again. They are unable to adapt to a new situation without completing another program because the programs developed at those institutions are designed to respond to a clearly defined, technical need and only that particular need.

Practical adaptability is also a clearly defined skill; not only that, it is a skill that can be taught. This is the opportunity that liberal arts institutions must embrace. Practical adaptability is not accessible to those who simply become a practitioner of many things. It is gained by understanding the kinds of transitions that our world requires workers to make, and liberal arts institutions must make it their task to prepare our graduates to thrive in those challenging times. While practitioners need to be led from one task to the next, liberal arts graduates must be able to anticipate the coming need. While practitioners are unable to see how their skills are relevant, liberal arts graduates must be ready to redefine the problem in a digestible manner. And while practitioners realize that their education did not teach them how to solve problems that require just a "two degree" shift in thinking, liberal arts graduates will only be able to lead if they are provided with an understanding of how their fundamental knowledge was applied across a diverse array of practical experiences.

This is currently more of a challenge for liberal arts institutions than one may expect. Liberal arts institutions have been allowed to exist so independently of the environment its customers enter upon graduation that it is often difficult to understand the fundamental partnership that must exist in order for both to be successful. The partnership is not a servant-master relationship as exhibited by practitioner-focused education, which it is often argued for by those who are commoditizing education. The partnership is not an employee-employer relationship that can often be found in research institutions. The key to a successful liberal arts education is the discovery process. It is the process that is often taught to entrepreneurs as "lean" or "customer discovery." It is not about taking a theory and overbuilding an unusable solution. It is about seeing the simplicity of the world. There is no hidden trick. The problems of the world are there for all to see if we are willing to look. The liberal arts institution must give us enough access to the world in the context of the fundamentals we are exploring that we know what we are seeing.

Community collaboration

Our graduates become little more than the prisoners in the Allegory of the Cave when hubris forsakes community collaboration. Unless our students are provided direct engagement, their knowledge remains deceptively incomplete. Whether defined by geographic proximity or digital connectivity, many of our liberal arts institutions are economic drivers in their community. In the small towns around them, they are the largest employers of highly paid employees. In the alumni networks made up of their graduates, they are the source of employment and partnership opportunities. And in their institutional networks, they are the intellectual complements that can lead to collective ingenuity. Liberal arts institutions are charged with the mission of ensuring that their graduates are fit upon graduation to become contributing members of society. The completion of this mission requires us to understand society through our communities.

In the same way that liberal arts institutions cannot have a slave-master or employee-employer relationship with industry, neither do they have a sage-pupil relationship with the community. Effective collaboration results instead in a joint partnership that shares burden. The burden of the community is to choose its path. Choices like these can only be taken by those who take responsibility for the consequences of those choices. While liberal arts institutions in themselves can be supportive, the value of this support is minimized if it is perceived as leading. The burden of the liberal arts institution is to provide sufficient options — options that must be assessed within a world of intellectual freedom based upon fundamental knowledge and contextualized in reality. The institution itself can never be the sage as much as it should be the source for those who have been intimate with enough decisions that those experiences someday drive their own informed choices.

Like a sociologist who must walk the fine line between active observation and influencing involvement, a successful liberal arts education provides access that is tempered by an understanding of its limitations. Liberal arts institutions are the resources that ensure those who on their way toward ownership of their world have the support they need to achieve their goals, create their world, and develop their universe. Their institution cannot craft their universe for them, nor is it uniquely qualified to tell them what it should look like. Academia is little more than a reminder of what others have done before. And as extremely valuable as that resource is, the individual must have the ability and opportunity to do more. The individual must be prepared to understand where history ends and the possible begins. The individual must be prepared by the institution to accept value for what it is and the communities that make up our world for what he or she will make them to be.

Commit to value.

A liberal arts education that enables an individual to take an active role in civic life is highly valuable. Especially in our modern society where technology allows us to be effective technicians without fundamental knowledge, there is almost a greater need than ever before for individuals who are able to quickly adapt. We need individuals who are able to see an unrecognized complexity and ensure it does not remain unrecognizable. We need, as a society, to acknowledge our responsibility to help more of our citizens to become better human beings who can understand the human elements in both the causes and effects of technology enabled applications. Until that change in our collective consciousness occurs, our liberal arts institutions need to acknowledge where they provide value.

Technology has allowed for a commoditization of lecturers to the point where they should be considered no more than imperfect, multimedia versions of textbooks. The Yale Report of 1828 identified the need for entertaining lecturers in a world absent of technology. This was a world where YouTube did not exist to teach you everything from lawnmower repair to multi-differential calculus. In the context of this new technological reality with its cornucopia of sights, sounds, and visual effects, the lecturer lecturing becomes hopelessly ineffective. The data routinely demonstrates that there is a statistically significant increase in failure rate when instructors rely upon lectures as the primary mode of teaching. Most importantly, if we accept the premise that the role of the institution is to support a student on his or her path toward contributing to society, it should prompt us to ask: why do we lecture at all?

Lecture based learning, whether appropriately named or masked as "instruction," does provide educational value. But even taking into account those who gain value in this form of learning, a college cannot compete against the technologically enabled educational marketplace. From MOOCs to Google in general, society now has more data at its fingertips than ever before. The cost of commoditized lectures is lower and the quality is greater than at any point in human history. The liberal arts institution that continues to create and sell bespoke lectures against competitors who have perfected their commoditization is the modern version of General Motors verses Honda in the 1980s. If better lectures from better professors exist, it seems rational to buy those products and focus on the application of the data as opposed to competing to create incomplete data. If we are willing to acknowledge our fallibility with regard to our delivery of data, it opens us up to the creation of true value.

Define value

A product or service from a particular provider is considered a good value if it costs less than procuring something equivalent elsewhere. It is vital that any assessment of value is performed in the language of the customer, which is typically financial cost. Many liberal arts institutions believe obfuscation of cost will provide an opportunity to avoid discussion of programmatic tradeoffs. By not knowing what things cost, an expensive music program that supports high quality students will be safe from attack by a business program that accepts anyone willing to pay. In many cases, it is accurate that this obfuscation denies access to those difficult discussions and that we are missing structural realities that can lead to real opportunities.

Liberal arts institutions that are open to comparative cost analysis often believe that their educational fees or extra-curricular offerings must be competitive to similar institutions. Unfortunately, this is not the comparison being made by the customers we are competing for. Consumers want to ensure our institutions are both sustainable and world-leading. Regardless of who the customer is, the most valuable prospects are viewing the value of their time in the institution against the cost of procuring a similar effect in the "real world." This has not changed for at least a hundred and fifty years. What has fundamentally changed is the commoditization of what is historically viewed as the core product of our higher learning institutions: the lecture.

The following table uses approximations of average Midwestern costs to illustrate the type of comparison that a customer should be performing to assess the value of an educational institution. This comparison uses an average two-thirds to one-third allocation between lectures or instruction and tutorials or labs[11]; an hourly consulting rate of $150 per hour; and market averages for rent, food, drink, and entertainment within the general vicinity of the referenced institutions. It is not surprising that a liberal arts institution is able to provide room, board, and extra-curricular activities at a significant discount due to the fact that these services are procured in bulk verses retail. If we are surprised to see the total monthly cost in this comparison

---

[11] Informal surveys at private colleges in Iowa indicate that professors perceive this breakdown to be closer to 80% of time spent on lectures and only 20% of time being spent on student mentoring. When asking these same professors which efforts are more rewarding, the majority of respondents find greater reward in their time spent mentoring verses lecturing.

demonstrating the liberal arts institution as a better value than procuring the entire bundle of services in the "real world," it is because the way we characterize our product allows our customer to misidentify where our value abides.

Liberal Arts Solution	Monthly Cost	Differential	Monthly Value	"Real World" Equivalent
	$ 5,075	-4%	$ 5,280	
Lectures	$ 2,700	100%	$ -	MOOCs/Google
Tutorials/Labs	$ 1,300	-192%	$ 3,800	Consultants
Student Services	$ 75	-7%	$ 80	Clubs, gym, and rec sports
Room	$ 530	-32%	$ 700	Apartment
Board	$ 470	-49%	$ 700	Food and Drink

Our opportunity

Everything from the informational materials to the faculty expectations at the average liberal arts institution focuses on and is formed around lecture-based classes that are supported with discussions and testing. Because of this, our customers look at the fact that there are free data sources with equivalent or better content in the "real world" and so consider the entire institution overpriced. Acknowledging this comparison is the basis of the opportunity. As long as the argument remains about whether locally created and delivered lectures are better than MOOCs, the liberal arts education will continue to lose. As long as the argument remains about the campus community being more inclusive and fun than the "real world," the liberal arts institution will continue to lose. The opportunity to transform the perceived value of our institutions requires us to double-down on the guided analysis and tutelage that cannot be found anywhere else for an equivalent price. It is here, at its traditional roots, that the modern liberal arts education can be reborn.

More accessible data is created per year than has even existed over entire swaths of our collective history. Converting this flood of data into information and then applying that information to community solutions is difficult for even the most experienced individuals. For traditional college-aged students, this process is nearly impossible without guidance. Liberal arts faculty members are extremely valuable when they are able to focus on providing assistance to individuals striving to contextualize and effectively synthesize this data for use in information-based decisions. The resources at our liberal arts institutions offer the opportunity to provide this service at a cost that is far less than any "real-world" consultant's fees.

Our opportunity to reshape our actual and perceived value rests in our willingness to become community connected, project based, and consultant supported experimentation centers. We must be able to communicate to prospective students that the creativity they arrive with will drive their learning. We must be able to facilitate their learning through experiential opportunities, and we must ensure that the faculty are enabled to act as advisors for student experiences that are allowed the freedom to take the form of "real world" experimentation.

Expect commitment
This opportunity requires us to willingly examine the structural and cultural inertia that currently prevents

access to fundamental value. It is difficult for institutions to consider a course catalogue that is not based on classes that are created on campus. It is difficult to imagine a course syllabus that is driven by learning objectives instead of content milestones. It is difficult to institutionalize the convergence of interdepartmental learning opportunities within the standard "class." It is difficult to require teachers to become facilitators. But we must expect these things.

Success requires a structural commitment to reshaping how the institution operates. In many of our "experiential" classes, we still have students work in isolation. They are given a problem, they report out once or twice in 15 weeks with very little direct engagement with community experts, and they are then assessed on a final report when it is too late to correct any deficiencies. This process is tedious for the professionals that engage, useless for the students themselves, and an overall waste of time for the institution if the purpose is to provide the student with more than a tick box toward achievement of an unmarketable degree. Collaboration does not materialize through momentary colocation. All partners must share integrated, iterative objectives.

Commitment requires an alignment of our expectations and rewards. We must expect that our faculty use the lowest cost data sources, whether it is their lectures or someone else's. We must expect that our faculty create fluid, responsive learning environments that rate success in demonstrated competencies instead of regurgitated content. We must expect our faculty to build collaborative learning environments that include groups of students focused on different aspects of the experiential learning opportunity. We must expect that our faculty see their role as facilitating the synthesis of information instead of the discovery of data, and we must reward those who meet these expectations as aggressively as we remove those who are denying our institutions' customers access to the value of a liberal arts education by idealizing a dream to the point of missing the opportunity. By institutionalizing this expectation, we will set the institution on a path of revitalization.

Embrace the journey.

The challenge of achieving value in a liberal arts institution is the fact that self-discovery does not have a timetable. Accepting the purpose of the liberal arts institution is an act of accepting that a graduate is not a fully formed product. The liberal arts institution is not molding clay; it is helping the individual gather the tools required to assemble his or her own version of a fully formed universe. This process does not stop at graduation, and embracing the journey as the purpose makes it difficult to assess success in the short term.

Further, the commoditized educational system has been so effective in defining success as a financial return on investment that many are fighting back against financial measures of any kind in the misguided view that these are what have allowed us to lose sight of the journey. Success at its most basic level is a measure of ego, and our modern reality is that many people measure ego in terms of money. This is neither good nor bad. Many good people do many good things during their quest to acquire money, and others do not. Money is not an evil that must be fought, as many liberal arts institutions would attempt to argue. A liberal arts institution should not be ashamed by graduates who are successful in their pursuit of money and should not be afraid of being judged by the financial performance of its graduates. It must be realistic, however, in the fact that no isolated measure of an individual's universe can ever gauge success.

The liberal arts institution succeeds when the customer realizes that the institution was responsible for enabling him or her to affect the trajectory of his or her destiny. In the same way that capitalism is perverted by corporations that seek quarterly profits over long term value, the Yale Report of 1828 clearly acknowledges that a liberal arts education is debased when its value is defined by a student or parent who has yet to understand the value of the product. We have spent generations assuming the customer is the student and that the institution solves problems he or she alone cannot hold.

Customer discovery
In any successful enterprise, it is the customer's problem that is solved. Within the context of a liberal arts institution, the student is the one who begins his or her journey of discovery with the help of the resources available through the institution. But if the liberal arts institution is serving its purpose, the student is not the only customer. This journey of discovery cannot occur without community interaction. It cannot occur without corporate engagement. It cannot occur without alumni

direction. These are often seen as contributors to the successful delivery of products and services for the student, who is often seen as the solitary customer.

This conclusion that the student is the sole customer is most common in institutions that begrudgingly accept the theory that tuition purchases a degree that demonstrates the qualifications of the student; the community is getting volunteers in exchange for experiences that benefit the student; or companies are paying for meeting space that helps reduce cost for the student. This belief influences everything from how we recruit to how we assess faculty to how we identify successful outcomes.

The very nature of the liberal arts institution is to synthesize superficially disparate items. How does a capitalistic society protect the weak? How do we find science in religion? How do we integrate technology and nature? This synthesis often remains elusive when one component is a customer and everything else is a service provider. The institution must be designed to provide value to all those whose contributions define the performed synthesis. And this synthesis must be recognized as requiring continual engagement. This synthesis cannot exist until we expand the focus of our services to include customers we are undervaluing and underserving.

Each institution has built strengths and weaknesses over its generations of existence. These must be acknowledged in the customer discovery process, yet they must not be allowed to define our vision. We must be willing to pull back to first principles and see where we are adding fundamental value and where we are attempting to chase institutions that are not actually our competitors. We must be willing to reexamine all facets of our services, all customers — recognized or not — and all revenue models. For example, why do we admit "revenue units" defined by the value of student tuition and fees? What if we admitted students with the view that they are more akin to "equity investments" that mature as a function of their professional value? Taking stock of what we do best, who we do it for, and how it could be monetized will allow us to look beyond the present to find a sustainable future.

Institutional impact
Our institutions are rarely designed to serve society. Our institutions are more often designed to assure a student that he or she will have the opportunity to become a professional. Our institutions are more often designed to exist alongside communities that could be engaged. Our institutions are more often designed to assure us that a path could exist toward meaningful civic engagement. We build a road up to the gate and allow people to find their path from there and then we ask them for more. We ask them to give when we are no longer serving them. We ask them to pay for the next generation, one that is not learning from their modern reality. We ask them to trust that, by chasing the whims of students, the institution will be serving the next generation.

In order to achieve the objective of preparing individuals for civic engagement, our integration into the surrounding world should be so complete that it is a primary function of the institution. The institution must facilitate the safe transition from the unknown to the possible. If we seek to serve the community defined by our alumni, we can do a better job of ensuring that our students will have the ability to build from the "real world" instead of being defined by it. Unfortunately, we rarely have a community relations office that is designed to better our community through partnership. We often assemble engagements that are very transactional in nature. We provide service to parallel communities as extra workers on cleanup days. We build internship offices that place students in confined roles where they cannot cause too much damage in exchange for being located nearer the "real world." We provide tuition kickbacks to public service clubs that perpetuate the misconception that community service is inherently sustainable. We do not put in the hard work of ensuring our students understand that serving the customer will always be hard work.

We spend more time visioning *what we want to be* than we spend looking at *what we are*. It is difficult to accept a frank appreciation of the outcomes we are driving, where we are unexpectedly succeeding, or acknowledging where we may be yet unable to compete. Our alumni define the institution, and theirs is our community. We must seek out their needs in order to define and institutionalize our solutions. We must understand that to serve our customer is to serve our alumni first, since theirs is the world our students are preparing to inherit. The institution must become a partner in alumni efforts to shape their world, a world they must continue to adapt, reinvent, and repurpose themselves. As an institution, in order to have our intended effect, this means deemphasizing the offices that seek more from the external world and expanding those that deliver externally.

Event horizon
Our current product is typically encircled by a four year event horizon, but our customers require services over a lifetime. We tend to focus on performance within this envelope and assessment of a student's state upon departure. We support two diametrically opposed positions; we are preparing students for an undefinable future, yet we are able to define their success through their preparation. The effort of institutionalizing our service to our customer by focusing on the communities created by our alumni means we must also look beyond the artificial event horizon encasing our current institutions.

Removing this event horizon forces us to reassess the way we assess. Most importantly, it opens us up to the possibility of refocusing *who* we assess. For example, when our professors are assessed by the individuals the professors are assessing, there is an inherent opportunity for collusion that serves no one. We would not expect someone who is running their guts out on a treadmill to appreciate the treadmill until they step off of it. Why do we believe, given human nature in the context of our desire to avoid discomfort, that achieving a fair assessment of an educational process is any different? If we plan to receive the feedback necessary to continually improve the institution, we must not only integrate the community in the process but, more importantly, the community must lead the assessment of the process's utility.

A shift in focus from assessing the activity to assessing the outcome can be scary. It initially creates a feedback lag and structurally removes control from those who have historically taken comfort in their ability to affect the outcome of their assessment. It devalues academic transparency and emphasizes individually driven achievements. It depowers those who have mastered the art of collusion and requires that effort be focused on motivating unpredictability. It requires the institution to put its trust in the concept that it will be judged on its present in the future by embracing the present it created in its past. It requires us to share the journey of our alumni and, through that partnership, embrace the future.

By embracing a future that focuses on mentoring citizens as they grow to shape their own universe, we will arrive back at a modern implementation of the true Socratic principles that originally defined a liberal arts education.

Part II: Engage

Achieving this focus is not simple, but it is also not impossible. Each institution will have specific challenges that can be solved by engaging small, specific, structural adjustments. Presented here are a few of those achievable, transformative changes. While the "devil is in the details," and each institution will require its own unique procedural strategy for implementing transformative change, tangible objectives are crucial.

Everyone loves progress but hates change. Success requires that innovation look familiar.

Recruit teams.

Liberal arts education creates the "stem cells" of our world. These stem cells are the influential community members who can quickly and effectively take the shape of any tactical form or function. Their creation occurs when we design educational systems, train facilitators, and embrace the socioeconomic diversity needed to achieve depth through breadth. Without a broad understanding of the tertiary elements around a topic, its true depth cannot be understood. This same principle applies to the teams we build that become our institution.

Recruiting at a liberal arts institution is typically done with a "big funnel." Big funnel theory assumes both your conversion rate and value per student remains constant, so revenue will increase proportionally to the number of candidates you engage. This concept has two perceived benefits: First, it provides recruiters with objective enrollment targets. Second, it is compatible with the assumption that any liberal arts institution is nimble yet robust enough to serve anyone.

No football program says, "Give us anybody and we'll figure it out when they get here." Coaches have particular skills, programs have particular histories, and the goal is to effectively match all of the various components into a team that has the best opportunity to win games. While sports teams are now using complex Portfolio Theory style algorithms to define success and pursue undervalued recruits, these techniques are being largely ignored by the institutions that are perfecting these methods. Driving lifelong partnerships between the institution and its students requires us to refocus our recruiting techniques.

So where do we start?

Hire sales professionals,
Successful sales professions create human connections while rigidly adhering to standardized engagement and communication procedures. Knowing your product is not enough; being eager is not enough; and looking the part is not enough. Selling is a discipline and recruitment is sales. We must stop believing that a young, attractive, underpaid graduate who loves the institution is enough. We must hire recruiters as sales professionals first. We must then refine their skills to the point where they have every opportunity to succeed and hold them to the same exacting standards of any sales professionals. Students should be coming for the professors, the research, or the cultural opportunities, but a professor is not, and need

not be, an expert at closing the deal. An institution's recruiters must be up to that challenge.

From and based in the market you want to sell in,
People buy from people who they know and like — people they trust. No one buys from a car salesman who looks or feels like a car salesman. The top performers are always the people who feel like a brother, an uncle, or a friend. Anyone who is selling a product needs to be a reflection of the customer rather than the product. When young recruiters spend over thirty weeks per year flying to the customer, they reflect a product to which people cannot relate. Instead of spending significant amounts of money to send "foreigners" into cities that they do not know, we should look at hiring sales professionals who live in the target market. We cannot successfully send star-struck, small-town Iowans to the big city of Boston and expect someone from Milton Academy to take them seriously. To sell to Milton Academy, we must hire individuals who have lived in the Milton Academy community, who can communicate in that community, and who can sell the unknown to other people in that community — people who know and trust them. If we hire recruiters who live in our target regions, who know their customers, and who visit our college once a quarter to learn about the product, rather than paying for recruiters who do not know the customer to be on the road until they burn out, we can reduce cost and improve outcomes.

Targeting strategic fit.
It is antithetical to a liberal arts education to believe an individual with perfect grades and perfect test scores is

the optimal customer for every college. A significant portion of straight-A students in our "no child left behind" world are boring, uncreative, and skilled only at staying quiet until someone gives them the right answer. This is not a revelation. It is discussed on many of our liberal arts campuses. If we know these individuals' skills are limited to a traditional academic achievement model that does not reflect the core of a liberal arts education, why do we continue to invest so many resources in pursuit of these individuals? If our local salespeople are selling our core product — professors who are there to guide individual discovery in a tutorial-based environment — we should be actively adjusting price based on the value of that product for that candidate. For example, the tutelage of a math professor at an institution that is consistently turning out graduates who enter executive tracks at the world's largest insurance companies should not need to offer a discount. Alternatively, a music program with no graduates of note and limited job prospects may need to ask for a lower price in order to ensure a sufficient return on investment for the customer. Portfolio theory does not require every asset in the portfolio to be a winner. If we dynamically mix the costs and revenues associated with our basket of offerings based on the varying quality of the tutelage each professor can provide, we can begin strategically recruiting for profitability.

Provide neither equality nor fairness but access to both.

Many professors are not ready to accept that the modern world has redefined the areas in which they create value as educators. Many are uncomfortable accepting the fact that the lecture has been commoditized to the level of an interactive textbook. Many are uncomfortable knowing they can no longer regurgitate a textbook to make it through another semester. Many are uncomfortable moving from dictating a path to supporting a random walk. These transitions become impossible if the assessment mechanisms are not revamped.

The current professorial assessment model in many liberal arts institutions is essentially unacknowledged collusion. In an attempt to be "student centered," many liberal arts institutions have been increasing the weight of student assessments in faculty review processes. This increase allows some professors to internalize a direct connection between job performance and student happiness. This connection, once made, provides both the professor and the student access to individual rewards for collectively diminishing the institution's academic standards. If an institution intends to implement strategies that push the classroom further from standardized testing and structures toward a tutorial-based system, this student and professorial assessment model has to change.

Successful assessment requires an acknowledgement of the objectives. We need to be sure we are assessing appropriately for the type of education we want to provide. If our intent in a modern liberal arts institution is to enable individuals to take an active role in civic life, a reward system must be built around an assessment of that core objective.

But where do we start?

Implement alumni review boards,
Much like a treadmill, you cannot possibly assess the quality of your liberal arts education until after you have completed it. There are few people who, while pushing themselves to exhaustion on a treadmill, start thinking about how much they enjoy the treadmill. The treadmill is a tool that causes controlled stresses that an individual must overcome in his or her quest for improvement. Allowing the individual, the individual being improved, to rate the workout while it is occurring is a meaningless and, if taken too far, a dangerous tool for eliminating your best professors. At the same time, reliance on peer reviews fosters a culture of protectionism because no one wants to be too hard on someone else when that individual will soon be in a position to judge. Therefore, an alumni review board would be the best group to be tasked with understanding the effectiveness of an institution's educational techniques and be incentivized to hold individuals accountable for the betterment of the institution.

Industry grading panels,
An underlying theory driving our reliance on standardized testing is that the teacher is unable to be both an advocate for his or her students and an impartial analyst of their performance. Standardized testing is

suitable for some disciplines like engineering (e.g., in project-based engineering, either your design performed the required task or it did not), but even when looking at advanced engineering degrees where topics can get more subjective and the advisor takes on a role of tutor, outside professionals assess the quality of the work to avoid bias. In a modern liberal arts institution, where the quality of one's real world performance is the desired outcome, we create a fundamental confrontation when we combine the roles of coaching and assessment within the responsibilities of the professor. If we find topical experts within our alumni review boards, much like we do for a peer reviewed journal, we will have a better chance of grading the student against the expectations of the real world without compromising the objectivity of the professor.

To assess professor performance.
Using alumni for assessing both professor and student performance enables independent evaluations of faculty effectiveness that are informed by real world needs or applicability. In addition to increasing alumni involvement, developing these structures will allow professors to focus on instruction techniques that produce long term results verses short term happiness. Combined with a long-term contract structure instead of traditional tenure, like one where a professor may be afforded multiple years to correct any identified deficiencies, utilizing the evaluations of individuals who are affected daily by the long term quality of that professor's instruction will provide meaningful responsiveness. This approach of elongating an

alumnus's contact with the institution, lagging the evaluation period for assessing effectiveness, and focusing assessment on real world applicability will allow the professor to be the coach and the institution to be the treadmill that together enable better citizens.

Focus on the long game.

Liberal arts institutions often find themselves trapped in believing they are building pathways to graduation. These institutions see the high school student, who is often backed by parental financing, as the customer who is ready to complete a liberal arts degree as cost effectively as possible. While we acknowledge that further education or training will be relevant, the product we assume our customers seek is the piece of paper in the diploma holder. We define their goal as to complete enough courses to graduate, and we debate value or results based on an institution's ability to drive completion of these structured steps.

Life is unstructured. There is no scoreboard. There are no midterm grades, no final exams, and no Dean's list. The liberal arts education allows individuals to make sense of this world, determine how they will fit into it, and create a scoring system that is meaningful for them. Some will choose cash as the value mechanism; some will choose non-profit board positions; some may even choose LinkedIn skill recommendations. All are equally meaningful in the big picture, and the role of the liberal arts institution is to help each individual find the right, unique path.

This process does not occur over three or four years. It is not complete by the age of twenty-two. Humans continue to evolve throughout life. Humans seek guidance in *all* stages of life, and the liberal arts institution should be available in all of those stages. If we are successful at engaging alumni in our effort to craft an effective learning environment, those individuals will care far more about the meaningfulness of the resume that is facilitated through the educational process than the letter grades attributed to the supporting research undertaken in class. If our alumni define their own successes, we must ensure that the institution is focused on making them successful.

But how do we focus on this?

Focus on career placement,
For those alumni who seek out financial success, the institution is valuable if it helps them land a well-paying job. For those who measure success in the roles they take, the lives they affect, or the meaningfulness of their networks, the institution is best remembered for what it did to effect that outcome. Very few pizza delivery boys look at their student loan debt payment and remember Introduction to Sociology fondly. Successful alumni who are more actively engaged with the institution as alumni hire recent graduates, donate time back to the institution, and give money to its fundraising campaigns. If alumni judge the value of the institution based on where they are years after graduation, the institution must focus on getting them where they want to be in the years that follow that May or December ceremony. This

means investing in career placement, not just career readiness.

Not entry level employment,
Most colleges have career services departments, and nearly all of them focus on job placement following graduation. From career fairs to onsite recruiters, this focus on finding employment nearly always assumes the job they get will not be their final job. Many of these jobs are sought out as stepping stones before graduate school or work experience take them elsewhere. We offer services under the expectation that we open doors for graduates, but the focus of the institution should be on constructing a pathway. The most valuable time for us to effectively step back into the lives of our alumni, the time in which they will look at the contribution of the institution and remember that they must give back to an organization that gave so significantly to them, is decades after graduation.

Focused on executive recruiting.
A career services department whose professional job placement specialists are staffed and focused proportionately to the career stage of the alumni it should serve will benefit the modern liberal arts institution the most. For every graduate who comes out of a liberal arts institution this year, there are twenty alumni of that institution who will be seeking executive level employment. By focusing on this segment of our alumni, we are helping to place them in a better position to contribute to the institution. We are putting them in a better place to hire liberally, contribute strategically, and donate significantly. Our alumni network should be a

wealth of warm leads, friendly partnerships, and actionable conduits. Executive recruiters who attempt to fill everything from board seats to C-suites spend generations attempting to build what could be activated by the career services department of a liberal arts institution. By focusing on serving our alumni at the time they need it most, we build wealth by reexamining when our alumni need value.

Share the risk.

The magnitude of educational debt is frequently cited as one of the Millennial generation's greatest challenges. Many are leaving higher education owing more than an average house, but are being paid annual salaries that are less than their annual tuition fees. This return on investment will improve with the implementation of a strong strategy for finding actionable value in the institution. However, for recent graduates, the magnitude of the debt is rarely the issue.

The challenge affecting Millennials is not the size of the debt but the monthly payments they must put toward that debt. The strain of these payments is immense at the beginning and miniscule even a decade late, especially for liberal arts graduates who plan to complete more schooling or build up to their potential within the workplace. We know this is the case. We see it every day. Our institutions are designed to facilitate this career path. If that is the case, and if we believe our institutions are performing as intended, why don't we offer a royalty-based payment plan?

If we truly believe the product will lead to long-term returns, why don't we put our money where our mouth is? Instead of creating debtor relationships between our alumni and our institution, why not make equity investments in our prospects? If alumni opted to pay less than 9% of their salaries to the institution instead of paying student loans for thirty years, the average Midwestern liberal arts institution would have all of its costs covered. It could then admit students who are right for the institution instead of only those who can pay the cost of tuition. It could remove its dependence on Federal programs that constrain educational innovation. It could allow alumni to repay that investment as a function of their ability, and it could allow the community to share in its success.

But how do we get started?

Find market rate,
Our programs must cost what they are worth. Combining strategic recruitment with tracking operational overhead will make clear which courses enable graduates to receive the highest salaries, what campus opportunities best facilitate student engagement, and what characteristics or experiences make students and alumni the most valuable partners for the college. Modern technology has made this a straight forward exercise in cost tracking and data analytics. If a commercial real estate firm can track the value of each felt pad on a chair leg, a college can use those same techniques to characterize which students, departments, or programs create its most valuable long-term assets. We too often look at programs with a view

in favor of financial ignorance so we are able to avoid making difficult choices. The valuation data must be allowed to drive the price. From discount rates to recruiting targets, program costs must float as a function of program value.

Accept that cash is king,
The total size of your college debt is not an issue at the age of twenty-one in a job with an annual income of $25,000. The issue is loan payments that often exceed what would otherwise be considered disposable income. Most individuals who set the costs and payback terms do not remember what it is like when "cash is king" and you do not have enough of it. So while many private colleges go to great lengths to help save students 10% off of meals or $250 in books, these costs break down to pennies per month compared to the cash burden associated with current student loan payback terms. Instead of focusing on traditional financing methods, colleges would be better served if they combat tuition inflation by attacking the post-graduation cash flow implications for alumni.

Bet on your customer.
Any college that does not believe it has put its graduates into a position to succeed should not be in business. If we are selling potential students a belief that their investment will pay off, the college must be willing to demonstrate its belief in that pitch as well. If that is the case, the college should stop pushing students toward conventional, commercial loans. The college should offer equity-style financing that caps payments as a function of the graduate's salary. This strategy is not advocating

principal forgiveness or price reductions. Higher education would be underpriced if it were effectively focused. This strategy is, instead, advocating that the institution bet on its own sales pitch and reduce the near term cash effect on its graduates in favor of self-financing long term reimbursement. We are currently going after individuals who do not fit the focus of the institution and asking them to "pay more and trust us." We need to provide a service that is tailored in price and expectation to the right customer, as opposed to attempting to upsell the wrong customers into a product that is not designed for their end goals or objectives.

Betting on our target customers by sharing their financial risk is the first step that must be taken to ensure the modern liberal arts education is focused on achieving its potential.

In Conclusion

A liberal arts education is more important now than it has ever been at any other point in our history. Our world currently sees more fundamental changes per decade than previous generations saw in lifetimes. With each new technology comes the obsolescence of the last generation's technologists. And within each wave of obsolescence comes a greater appreciation for our society's "stem cells," individuals who have learned the skills of rapid adaptation inherent in their liberal arts education.

For centuries now, liberal arts institutions have been nudged further and further away from the principles of a liberal arts education. The aggregate effect of these continual nudges towards academic standardization, student happiness, or community service is often a gulf separating tuition cost from societal value. Where this has occurred, the institution is often searching for ways to save the institution – offering solutions in search of problems, and inadvertently debasing the liberal arts.

Rediscovering the modern value of our liberal arts institutions requires that we face more than just the questions or consider more than just the solutions presented herein. But if this manifesto can help us to again see the institution as a vehicle and society as the customer, our modern liberal arts education can return to its historic, fundamental purpose: *to enable individuals to take an active role in civic life.*

About the Author

Chris Draper is Director of EMERGE, a venture accelerator started at Simpson College in Indianola, Iowa. The EMERGE "Incubator in a Box" network allows traditional entities – small private colleges, rural city governments, regional economic development associations – to provide its members the infrastructure to grow local entrepreneurial opportunities without shouldering unreasonable economic burdens. Built around a dynamic equity operational model, the EMERGE economic gardening strategy has enabled over 500 individuals to invest nearly $1,000,000 of value and create over 25 part time jobs supporting more than 45 pre-seed and early stage ventures during the first two years operating in a community of less than 16,000 people.

An engineer by training and entrepreneur by accident, Chris is an operations expert who serves as a board member, advisor, or investor for startups, non-profits, and traditional businesses that focus on topics or products ranging from biofuels trading to performance arts, STEM education to labor negotiation. This manifesto calls upon his experiences working with small private colleges from across the United States that struggle to regain sustainability within a "new normal," and identifies the thought process that led to implementable solutions like EMERGE.

Chris received his Bachelor of Science in Mechanical Engineering from the University of California at Berkeley and his Doctor of Philosophy from the University of Glasgow in Glasgow, Scotland.

Made in the USA
Middletown, DE
21 March 2016